Penitential Cries

Books by Susan Howe

Available from New Directions

The Birth-Mark

Concordance

Debths

The Europe of Trusts

Frame Structures: Early Poems 1974–1979

The Midnight

My Emily Dickinson

The Nonconformist's Memorial

Pierce-Arrow

The Quarry

Sorting Facts: or 19 Ways of Looking at Chris Marker

Souls of the Labadie Tract

Spontaneous Particulars: Telepathy of Archives

That This

Penitential Cries

Susan Howe

A New Directions Paperbook Original

Design by Leslie Miller
Manufactured in the United States of America
First published as New Directions Paperbook 1645 in 2025

Library of Congress Control Number: 2025030274

2 4 6 8 10 9 7 5 3 1

New Directions Books are published for James Laughlin
by New Directions Publishing Corporation
80 Eighth Avenue, New York 10011

CONTENTS

Penitential Cries 9

Sterling Park in the Dark 29

The Deserted Shelf 83

Chipping Sparrow 89

PENITENTIAL CRIES

Therefore, they shall be as the morning cloud, and as the early dew that passeth away, as the chaff that is driven with the whirlwind out of the floor, and as the smoke out of the chimney.

Hosea 13.3

Each morning rapid heartbeat. Scattered alphabet

Hello Interloper the Fake

Standing on the brink of afterlife or nothing

Little relation to everyone more open and free. Designedness.
Quietness and alacrity of soul running parallel

thinking it is too late to try for art to bring out peace

Somebody Else

Amen

Watercolor pencil series thirty-six colors pale red to grey hidden
watercolor brush under the lid

What colors of the spectrum express perfection

Let mind wander over prehistoric combat. All the kingdoms. Egyp-
tology Europathy Sinology cold and hot then annihilation, cast out
land of spirit-world anterior to creation even fishes

some indecipherable leaping

Widows and Pariahs 1

I woke up this morning half out of a dream and thought *Widows and Pariahs* was a good title—for to be one or both is to be anonymous in soft rain on a quiet street waiting quietly alone. We feel even more alone Saturday and Sunday. Nevertheless, in suburb twilight there is happiness in listening before leaving the simplicity of life, no matter what supernatural messages are nesting in physical therapy and distinguishing marks. Frailty means nothing Night of my soul, not yet forced to go paperless, branches and brilliance, willing to run the risk of whistling dust beside lists of other authors and what admiration and affection means disclosed to a worldwide interpreter who whispers low in each baby's ear no one knows what chrism in cradle. Little wandering sonic Juvenilia formed to body likeness you seek nothing but authentic substance, still depths of the mighty forest. Thank you love of the sea under whose breaking waves

Enjambment tipped in with wings extended

before forgetting the intellectual part not even two syllables not the least sting in the arm—sometimes even exultation

Hello Usurper

There remains a root of bitterness in the best hypocrites. You have your reward.

One generation falling asleep. Another waking up

Pontiff of the Sun, and of Vesta, Augur, Quindecemvir, Hierophant, &c. &c. I suppose creation and not wishing to go out and the stars left open is that why the old man with the beard was in the Roman mosaic floor of a building site in London, well they have a history so do we. Speeches about the concept of an Academy in America. Greetings from the other Academy etc. Motives are different still beating heart tell all

Miles away as the crow flies

Developers are erecting a scaffold for a spec house on Main Street where the Stony Creek Post Office used to be. I climbed over the frame structure and told a carpenter there to call David even if he was dead already.

Ghost Walk footsteps rustling across sins of ancestors

Sheet rock second stories collapsing in on us

"Why do the nations so furiously rage together, and why do the people imagine a vain thing?"

Whining drones. My head is gone.

I have wept away all my brain

I went around and around the way I had come. Cold War heating up

Cold as religion covered in snow

"Heretical woman, what God wills when will is lost is nothing compared to what you will never know. You cannot have what God wills you should will hereafter"

Hush Angel of Revelation, brandishing a sword in right hand striding across myriad minimum long gone pension funds.

Don't worry. You have met your deductible and can check in at one of our Welcome Kiosks before headlong drop to earth whether gold or no

Light rain outside little taps or clicks on skylight. Guardian L'Ange Heurtebise, in search of poetry 1950. Jean Cocteau, panes of glass on his back, 1889–1963. Eurydice, lay your body on photo paper exposing it in such a way from one horizon at the edge of underground routes not taken, fawn to pulse brittle tape recording contained in metal holder. Razor blade, slicing block. Work cut out. Cégeste killed in the war.

"Look at yourself in a mirror all your life and you'll see Death at work like bees in a hive of glass."

1916 Eastern Front Southern Galicia now Ukraine Ludwig Wittgenstein on his WWI German Army night watch bird nest observation-post artillery tower. Tall as the Ladder of Perfection. Touch his wounds with a blossoming rose.

It's too late now worship of the Wounded Side. Ruins, bombs, corpses, fragment letter-bits, the veins of a poem hemmed in humanity reach all things below as never was.

Save a bit of breath before and after

War is constant. During the Vietnam War time, when radio programs were produced using analog tape machines, I produced and edited recorded poetry readings at WBAI housed in a deconsecrated Swedish Evangelical church on East 62nd Street. The recording booth was monitored by an engineer. Our smaller editing booth was soundproofed and padded, the door was padded except for a small glass window so looking out you saw people walking around outside: visitors, performers, composers, conductors, politicians, poets, all lips and eyes.

We had a steel editing block with a flat groove intersected by a thin vertical edge for splicing with a single-edge razor. There was an overhead light because we needed to follow the rhythm of breath of each reader in order to pick up the next word, following with a bit of breath to ride the feedback. When WBAI FM was short on funds, we re-purposed tape spools that were erased. Often under the surface splicing and reconnecting I became aware of quick pshpshphsh hesitant alphabetic ghost difficulties hurrying along their apparitional way

All our fellow prisoners salute that little part we have in you alone among originals, sinner born virtuous to do good

Fear not the millstone.

Patchwork flower decorum. Nothing too little to escape attention, Small hand with index finger extended to mark out places that call for vengeance

Creation and perfection.

Printing is so divine a nature it flies into cemetery plots of a world without nearness

Poetics of space I know it must be about 5 am.

Death entered the world because of sin.

An octogenarian from another dream state offered to take me home. I followed him to the timetable. There were crosses on the numbers. I knelt and held on because every sentence, heeding the call must come to an extremist edge. Not only phonemic, but a graphic force field representing the critical spirit in its order and ruthlessness, is following each comma to ecstasies of exactness. Not in a Capitalist sense but in the retirement sense.

To Whom It May Concern, It's time for an update. Insertion of needle into vein for collection of blood sample deeper than ruins are

I've been lucky I say to the indifferent universe

"There is a great river this side of Stygia"

Geriatric tachycardia murmurs *pounding or fluttering even chaotic*; an echocardiogram can only tell so far

7:15 am. It's hard to make out the numbers on my watch because it's an ordinary Timex with a small face under glass and a narrow leather strap made to fit around a widow pariah's thin arm while the Connecticut River flows to a cosmic unknown place where the "elderly" get lost. "The River of Rivers in Connecticut," Wallace Steven's great poem, is a poem of resignation. "'The river is fateful, // Like the last one. But there is no ferryman. // He could not bend against its propelling force."

Marguerite Porete says she cannot have what God wills she should will. For her, will is nothing compared to the fullness she will never be given, and this is the will of God. Love has her in captivity so strongly she wills nothing, so I keep telling my heretical paper self to get up and write this down by dawn's occult twilight when morning has come and night is crossing over somewhere posthumous to tell the hush truth

Widows and Pariahs 2

We were readers each in our Separatist groups. Mine had discovered dreamers and secret seducers of souls wrapped in gender-patterned penitence. The way a particular grain of paper speaks without our knowing to a leader in another sect scattering stars across a field running parallel with eternity the truth of quietness before birth of the world we need to run across to ask if nomen has other omens when each lost letter speaks for itself

Dear Health Care Provider,
I remember not remembering "bat, banana, apple" twice in the fifteen minutes allotted for my once-a-year Medicare Wellness Check. I didn't see a memory test for octogenarian pariahs coming and yes I admit the fact that I failed this first one is a bad sign but if only you had asked me to repeat "unanswered, perilous, question" after counting down from 47 backward in increments of seven. . . .

Womb of the morning

The tortoise isn't resting

Stand up facing the wall, chair behind you. Not feet splayed outward, you cannot go that low

Sooner or later Kindergarten is near

Slip: to convey secretly. To slide; to glide; to steal; to move along the surface of a thing without bounding, rolling, or stepping. To fall or sink into sleep. To go quickly and softly; to pass unexpectedly.

"Exquisite at her needle." Catherine Sloper—in the cloisters of Westminster Abbey, 1620.

Psalm 39:1: "I will take heed unto my Ways that I Sin not with my Tongue: I will keep my Mouth with a Bridle."

Bridal-knot

So much happiness in the little word "clasp"

*a*1639 H. Wotton *Reliquiæ Wottonianæ* (1651) 340 Julia a little before dying. Together with an infant she bare, ... and she gone without any slip remaining [etc.].

viz. divination by the gnawing of mice.

Other catch-all penitential pages. Cloth, eBook.

Gravedigger

Heretical woman almost dead soul—picking up memory threads requires courage. Do other recluse readers have vitae punctuated with references to enclosure

January 1742 Sarah Pierpont Edwards, alone in her room, tells what everlasting mountains God lifts above the Hell of her soul: "all persecutions & torments seemed meer nothing I seemd to ~~dwel~~ dwell on high: & the place of my defence to be the munitions of Rocks."

Tell: originally a mound or small hill; accumulated remains of ancient settlements. *Tell*: to give a narrative of facts. Johannes Kelpius 1667–1708, Hermit of the Wissahickon the Leader of the Society of the Woman in the Wilderness. Others of some note, as the story tells, have trod this wilderness.

"Stop walking over my grave go away and do something else."

Noah's dove returns not

We pass through an x-ray chamber to reach the airport terminal

Widows and Pariahs 3

Even if senses die down in old age and certain intensities are gone, my catastrophic thinking remains in place. Nevertheless I made an almost first post-Pandemic drive on I-95 from Guilford to Sterling Memorial Library in New Haven without a crash. This time I was hunting for Alvin Lucier's "So you (Hermes, Orpheus, Eurydice)," based on H.D.'s early poem "Eurydice," and Fintan O' Toole's *A Traitor's Kiss: The Life of Richard Brinsley Sheridan*. The wind was blowing so strongly I could barely get the heavy doors to the High Street entrance open what with the books I was carrying while clutching my cane. Once safely inside I passed along glassy walls of the new Poorvu Pedagogy Center for Teaching and Learning. The Center offers guidance on how instructors can adapt their teaching to ongoing developments in AI. Here various technology-enabled learning programs are distributed across muffled corridors of new money power. Crisis liquidity, well-mitigated risk, Ivy League endowments, notable portfolio adjustments, stakes in Alphabet incorporated, other bull markets

Orpheus pounds on the soundproof glass. He won't get through—he's mythical.

I passed through updated STEM-funded corridors and continued into Sterling's original faux-Gothic interior.

At the bookstack tower entrance, I tapped my plastic ID card and a thin slash of light turned green. The locked black padded door with brass buttons swung open. I climbed the narrow, twisting stairs, each step rimmed with nonslip tape so you can't slide in due time going up or down

"So you"

remember the gridded window placed at eye level like a peep hole in the door of a room in Boston's Massachusetts Memorial Hospital summer 1958 but here you can quickly escape. There are almost six and a half miles of shelves in the bookstack tower. Eurydice follows Orpheus from the underworld until restlessly he looks back to check.

I can see him in his ruthless certainty. What trespass to turn and see her face to face, ruining the desire in her to wander. She should remain hidden away like a family secret clothed in illegible moral syllables

Loyal to the least first phoneme in its never-to-be caughtness

"Hell must open like a red rose / for the dead to pass."

PS01-PS311. Corridor numbers are difficult for a retired researcher whose memory chain is rattling. Noumenon Disbelief Kant & Unknowability

Full particulars.

"Where'ere you walk cool gales shall fan the glade." Jupiter tells ensnared Theban princess Semele (future mother of Dionysus) his palace gardens will be paradise. "Trees where you sit; shall crowd into a shade"

Legato. *Fragile volatile foliage stitch-print stallion preamble*

Spiritual in cross-hairs. God knows where

"From a Woods ruines did these Buildings rise, And it stood Grove where now it Rafters lies."

Lovelace loveless lawless old English *laghless*. Names. Deer or gazelle the fact of our coming down from trees.

Limbo

"Look, look, what is that poem lying dirty under a bureau in the parlour /being used by maids to light / the fire?"

Melmoth the Wanderer

"The preacher paused, and a circle opening, disclosed the figure of a monk belonging to the convent, who stood among them.

* * * * *

* * * * * "

Tacking against the winds of time I can only cut and quote. Even here in the dark republic of mind and spirit where "Currer Bell" is a free human being with an independent will. Octogenarian widow pariahs genuflect as we trail across John Milton's shelves of blue ice. Glacier inside you might drop off his heart into the "world" he has given Eve; vain hopes, vain aims—

Jailor, bring the prisoner out, *now* is too late.

A distraught mother runs across the narrow corridor. "Where is he? Where is my boy?" She is in her fantastical role from a Theater of Somewhere Not Connecticut.

If you stand there long enough searching the half-empty shelves for John Donne's nineteen *Holy Sonnets* florescent tubular bulbs above switch off ever so quietly

Acousmatic peals of laughter, labials of instruments veiling their source

Exit landlord. Re-enter with two great coats.

Cordelia Clarissa

Our time is lost.

SML Truck inspection flag "going to deep storage."

John Donne, "My body my skin"

Textual apparatus against the coming cold. Skip the checkout desk. Return, and I will return to you, abolishing all fines and sins. No more cobweb curriculums. I'm sifting for sterling particles, delight of the hunt. Sometimes afternoon sun filters through tercet bone-dust, allophonic dust, pastoral watermark teething all *here*—all about the heart. The history of the world, a heap of refuse books, captivity, moments of birth and beauty, penitence, promiscuity, etc. One wise pariah of the mystic class going under the name of Spiritual peeps through an upper tower window-sliver into the center of the Starr Reading Room far below. She has left the metaphysical field as her work is not religious. Only an empty shell

Fresh Pond

Last night I dreamed I saw my mother sitting in the window of our house on the banks of Mount Auburn City with the old moon in her lap. Flesh of life returned from underworld. I knocked on the glass. "Don't do that! You startled me! Speak no more of these secrets you already know! Come in *now*, it's late!"

Phantom light

Supper is on the table our father lies full fifty fathoms five a storm is coming

—

Graduation Day. Immeasurable peace, sadness, love, and pity on earth. Harvest of clover, green meadows to walk across. I am here among my retired teaching colleagues. At long last we are going to throw off our battle fatigue. We have finished our tasks. Resigned what we thought we were meant to do.

Annihilated souls, we dwell in the field of the "beau fleuve," as it was called by Father Louis Hennepin, the first European to document the Falls. Their sailing-ship succeeded in reaching the Niagara River on 8 December, 1675. "The most beautiful and altogether the most terrifying waterfall in the universe." I know we will have to go back to Lethe meandering in ourselves because our world is falling away. We can only go so far as scattered sheep. Who will go first and who will come after. It was customary in 17th century Boston to cross the Charles River at fording places.

Morning. Early light where have they lain him? Mary come running the door is open the Lord is gone. We don't want to say goodbye even if we have to leave the "present" present with other groups of retirees, pariahs, and ancestral stutterers. It is up to us even if we are dead even if there is nothing in the tomb. I know this, but someone is waiting at the top of the steep hill covered in sand we must all climb to reach the lost family fable. It's easy, no pain in the knees, no poor balance, canes thrown away—when we finally arrive there is Lady Honoria Dedlock seated at her desk in Chesney Wold reading old love letters, even older than the ones our mother kept in a cardboard box beside the washing machine in the cellar. Children can see a thousand miles off

Heart pictograph little frills.

Personal and individual solemn forms appear we must hurry while tenderness survives in us secret languages cherished beliefs swimming in sun motes as if we had known then life expectancy or return to being ancient

Mitral tremolo sliding glissandi chaff

* * *

STERLING PARK IN THE DARK

Antiq

becoming for me; my long
now all of a sudden it is

Now we come
same origin as
we are actually
the so-called cc
large number o
not require muc
through the nat

(Poem)

have helped me: now all of a sudden

n ut of many leaves compacted
same strong growth impulse, it
to speak, with all its eyes in the
ch as possible; each small flower

10 9 8 7 6 5 4 3 2 1

sky ∧& sea[∧] of cobalt (

ich I retired into the (
have been mentiond o
:Came into my mind> >
th it is X that *86 <next y
e

te on my feet—o on my

I go this ~~px~~ ^a noon[^] to

s. These days are lovely

COMMENTARY
pp. 333–36); OQ
21–22); VA1 (ff.
(pp. 333–36); B (
28); F (pp. 125–

12mo, 1624

(ll. 51v–52

21–25); E (

–b (ll. 41–

Occasions,

confined.”] ~.^
phantom?] ~.
fact,] ~;

se I seemed t as it we
the ⊙ Concerning <m
strongly it Impressd o
thing in Heaven or Ea

390 Lie,] ~‸ 393

~‸ Downe;] ~‸ 39

~‸ it] him 403

400 flock] flocks

.e, Σ. showne.] H4 A

r); ~‸ Σ.

6. Prison] ~, C2 DT1

METEMPSYCHOSIS

I cannot tell you how readabl

efforts at deciphering, letter by

having its effect, and my quiet

Σ. Soule,] ~‸ Σ. hers] ~;

To ripen at long last to fruitful love!

of ~ H3(→ »~«).

~ others

ıe selfe truth and errs? nov
ı She,'and did She, and sh
on Seauen, or on no hill

like advent

n She
is m
And l
ay ki
first t
lls S,
one,
Doth
s Sh
pes

old place—full of the riche

the gentlest ups & downs &

surrounding landscape—a

dream of while absent.—T

kept safe and dry,

letter, have helped me

l had suc
~~ve me such~~
to [be] aliv
me> that
the Room

, ~~of the~~ which is
Help of the L
perfectly wean
the whole ⊙

ich from my mind every trace of human

O witches, O misery,

~~I can hear little voices whispering~~
~~O what are all the faint voices that I hear~~
What are the little voices ? I can hear
~~mournful & tender cries but not~~
~~fie~~ fine • [n *overwrites illegible letter*]

2

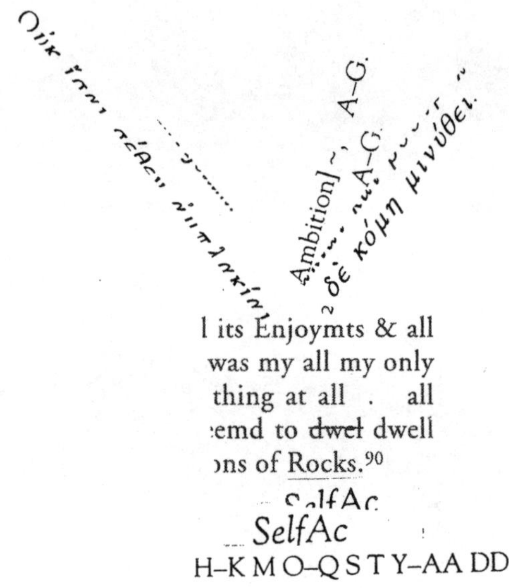
Ambition] ~, A–G.
δε κόμη μινύθει.
l its Enjoymts & all
was my all my only
thing at all . all
:emd to dwel dwell
ons of Rocks.[90]
SelfAc
H–K M O–Q S T Y–AA DD

~~serious bar to doing remunerative work~~

~~Cry out there~~

~~Cry~~

That ~~grand~~ unnumbered apple boughs; that grew

A Paraphrase of the Penitential Psalms

A–B D–F; ~^ H 3; Phriscus^

thee] ~, B45 H OC2 A–C 30;

*

OC2 SN3 A Phrine,] Phr

artifact

PENITENTIAL PSALMS

Tender & mournful cries but not the words

Introduction

Leaving | his en|terprise | with p

And there|in camp|*eth*, | spread

in the least even

in another. [. . .]

we sit in eternal

you — yet that,

Textual Apparatus

Then at | the root | it rag|eth o|ver all –
So far|eth love | when he | hath ta'en | a source:
His rein | is rage; | resis|tance vail|eth none;

So far|eth love | when he | hath ta'en | a source:
His rein | is rage; | resis|tance vail | eth none;

Leaving | his en|terprise | with p
And there|in camp|eth, | spreac
in the least even
in another. [. . .]
we sit in eternal
you—yet that,

Since that deceit || is ay returnable,
Of very force || it is agreeable
That therewithal be done the recompense.
Then guile beguiled || plained should be never
And the reward little trust forever.

Thirdly, there are those readers wh...
always strivi...

And when he saw that kindled was the flame,
The moist poison in his heart he lanced
So that the soul did tremble with the same.
And

A NOTE ON WYATT'S METRES

A Paraphrase of the ...

That those fair eyes had in his presence glanced,
The form that Love had printed in his breast

my thoughts that when I had
ent in this dark abode I used
Apotheosis Ignati,
ordinary age of man . upon
as not willing to be kept out..
s will Αὔξετ' ἀτασθαλίη, ἡ
<to answer> yes a thousand

–while I was speaking the words my mind s was help as it were flying out of my ~~Chaire~~ Chair was held down.

ıy soul seemed to be ın

God and to the Childre

ıtion & solace of soul

Earth at the feet of Gods s

ings with me & breath f

appear *[illegible]* far to

to get so far—& then I find,
loss to me to me which dra
, 3 1 9 7 4 3 3 2 6 6 .

EXIT.

(Ranunculus asiaticus),
too boastful of your beauty, once
in close embrace, but now two
'atered Ida holds. Orpheus prayed
.in to cross the Styx a second
ɔer drove him back.. Seven day:
he bank in filthy rags and witl
Care, anguish of soul, and tear
:nt, Complaining that the gods
.8 (f. 113v); H3 (p. 48); H5 (p. 4
.R1 (f. 279v); NY3 (f. [46v]); O21
.. 58); SN3 (f. 36v); VA3 (f. 78v); W

C (p. 69); D (p. 66); E (p.

ACORN

Acorn sprig
1530, Flor
* Sketches,

SIR THOMAS WYATT
176 It] I B7 CT1 DT1 H4(*ve*
B7 R1 ... DE5 H4 I
though

10 punishment.] ~, B7 B32 O20 SP1

LX Monte'
LX Hat C
LX Acorn
LX Eagle C
XC Crossbow
XC Star C
XC Star C
CI Anchor
CV Eagle C
CID Star B
CX Fruit C
CX Anchor
CX Anchor
CX Fruit C
CX Fruit C
CX Shears
CV Lamb C

h incompletely adapted leaf forms i:
le, the elm, the ash, and the birch) (
ee distinct rings of differently forme

9); C (p. 69); D (p. 66); E (p. 66); F (p. 66).

me about a month ago. I was going to the

evening – a dark evening, threatening thund

at the turn of the Heights, I encountered a li

a sheep and two lambs before him; he was cr

and I supposed the lambs were skittish, an

be guided. 58): SN3 (f. 36v): VA3 (f. 78v):

9); C (p. 69); D (p. 66); E (p. 66); F (p. 66).

HISTORICAL

they grow, see

TRANSITION TO F

"observation of the world"

place won't pay;
ehend is ^that[^]
m ∅ will prove r.

simply want elbow=room for the exer

I hope ~~for~~ ^during[^] the next ten year

certain importance; if I don't, it won't

...cessary

r'e genial, quoi! I would give all my unp

ritten "sleeps in an antre of that alp!" ar

custom of the land." & God's bright & ir

ns," & twenty other things in these & othe

se my ~~fate~~. ^mate.[^] Let us not fear, but lc

isfaction & confidence to a considerable ca

GENERAL INTRODUCTION

good!" And we talked

into silence & darkness,

system which he tried t

this act of yours which

+) · [) *overwrites* —]

devilty yet. My dear Stevenson, I delight in y
sense — it seems to me ‸impossible[‸] to posses
greater perfection than you do. You ~~ar~~ ‸have[‸]
poetic sensibility, but your'e so ‸monstrous[‸] c

9); C (p. 69); D (p. 66); E (p. 66); F (p. 66)·

ɔf poor Father's ~~going out~~ ^fading away[^]
the waves of the world closing over this
o offer it, & of how we were touched by
will (I am sure) do so much to rescue him

He remains in my mind as a

ı his ~~humanly~~ [^]humanity[^]

nner ~~of m~~ of the ⊙s treating the Children
in Prison And ~~found t~~ the thoughts of
ich attempts of their Enemies to make em
ne. it appeard astonishing folly that they
to hurt those who had such a Kingdom

~~I can hear little voices whispering~~
~~O what are all the faint voices that I hear~~
What are the little voices ? I can hear
~~mournful & tender cries but not~~
~~fie~~ fine • [n *overwrites illegible letter*]

105 Wayting] Watchinge B13 BR1 H8 O17; ~
B26. opened] (open'd) B13; ~, B32 C2 (
G; open, to BR1; openinge, H5; opening H
~) O17; op'ned VA2. day] ~, B32 BR1
~; H8 O20 SP1.

summer.[^] — [^]It is very late in the evenin
in the big dusky library of this institution,
& desolate at this period. I must go home &

Ever, dear daddy

I con *[inkblot]* tinued

Name upon nam

THE DESERTED SHELF

Prodigal Scribe after the readers are gone we are here but not. Before skeleton stone huts the sense of holiness and damnation at once all you need is an ash leaf or a four-leaf clover with word and music dancing at crossroads by the fishcold sea. Proteus of the deep sea ways. Come

If I had gone to college I wouldn't have to beg for admission every year with username and forgotten password. Evening of life

You can't. You can't return to the deserted shelf in your soul across miles of brown blanket bog and sand. Now one of us has shifted into "stage Irish" so we can understand the original without subtitles though better far

Five thousand years ago there was a huge open room with a long dining table at the far end and a peat fire and only a few volumes. We became close friends, though we'd never known each other before. You could bring along a sprig of hawthorn. It was a matter of sanctuary in simplicity

Deep sea fellow sentinels what is time to old King Priam standing on the battlements. Eurydice has drifted into Christian heresy, she is wandering from place to place with her flocks of sheep across eons and eons as if we can rest in emptiness for always

I did once try to write a cloud poem when suddenly I was shoved from the back. My multiauthor sammelband fell open and I thought, Wow! I have to get away from the medieval with its travail and tribulation. But what a feeling of God's quickening spirit while trying to remember one tresspass or another under its always closed cover turning to your neighbor as I am

I hope we will have talks here in constant assurance over the years of separation anxiety during the long winter breaks and odious February. We still have plenty of time to start over I could begin with previous publications spirit agglomerations missing comma however misspelled the encroachment

Justification without asking if humanly possible crossing the ocean with messages and Uilleann pipes playing *Caoineadh na dTrí Mhuire*. "Listen, mother, and do not be sorrowful." Summer 1958 booley village ruins under the slopes of Slievemore

Skipping pebbles across still water

Mary of Clopas stands in her chariot, she recognizes Ghost Cassandra in what is left, world of mortals from spilled tap water of eternity. Sometimes soil has a glow for all your barrenness you white witch ancestor, almost angelic a little on the raggedy side, uttering dry leaves to your last retirement slip. We have come to be familiar with our recently forgotten name. Sometimes in our memory chamber she looks like murder

Dynasty of mystics. What labor to live forever. Speak of the elect
what can you do in this world so much life in the little of it

Harold Hart Crane 1899–1932. Lost at sea.

Voyages VI "The Imaged Word, it is, that holds / Hushed willows anchored in its glow. / It is the unbetrayable reply / Whose accent no farewell can know." This stanza is a definition of what every single line in a poem is bound to promise and yes enjambment is ruthless as great expectation demands. Couplets clear the threshing floor

O my Prodigal, to swim the shadowy waters as a fish gone out

EPILOGUE

"Think not thou canst sigh a sigh / And thy Maker is not by; / Think not thou can'st weep a tear / And thy Maker is not near"

William Blake, *Songs of Innocence* 1789

Books weren't always struggling to believe in themselves. Drawn from mother's knee in ancient days of hallowed memory, long before astrological Familist, Ranter, Recusant-Apostate tracts; all Damn~~ationDivination~~—it's getting late. Trancendentalists huddle under their covers.

Mythbearer ~~Myrrhbearer~~

A dove for the Shaping spirit of Imagination beats her wings against two thousand tons of steel and iron built on early twentieth century skyscraper principles to hold sixteen miles of aisles with carrell partitions at windows.

CHIPPING SPARROW

for Fanny Howe

Left the body

Drowsd a little

Done with soul

–

What to think

Dusting up crown

Garment mirror

Pull me close

–

Quietness and calm

Rest and rejoice

No more doubt

Astonishing!

–

Bird and pencil dining

Bird and pencil dining

–

Special visitors

Walking on stilts
in snow
–

On the subject
of assurance

I should have
I should have
–

Self-scrap

Imagination
on the bias
–

Language of cold
Sitting beside sleep

Body as empty shell
–

When I came home

it was very late

There was little in

work but did go on

–

Civil fortification

years away~~away~~

whishth chipping

–

END NOTES

Grateful acknowledgment is made to Leslie Morris at the Houghton Library, Harvard University, for permission to use the cover image (MS Am 1118.5, B114), which is taken from an 1859 letter from Emily Dickinson (signed "Cole") to Susan Gilbert Dickinson. Volume II of *The Letters of Emily Dickinson* (Belknap Press, 1958) tells us that "pasted above the message is a woodcut clipped from Dickinson's copy of *The New-England Primer*." The cover art macrophotograph, taken by Jen Bervin, of "T" reveals in bleed through the other side of the page—"N": "NOAH did view / the old world & new." The letter runs:

> To Susan Gilbert Dickinson　　　　1859
>
> My "position"!
>
> Cole.
>
> P.S. Lest you misapprehend, the unfortunate insect upon the left is Myself, while the Reptile upon the *right* is my more immediate friends, and connections.
>
> As ever,
> Cole.

MANUSCRIPT: HCL (B 114). Pencil.
PUBLICATION: LL, where it is reproduced in facsimile facing page 156. The date is conjectured from the handwriting. Thomas Cole (1801–1848) was a well known American painter, and his name is here used to typify talent in sketching. Pasted above the message is a woodcut clipped from *The New England Primer*. The copy was a reprint made for distribution to all Yale graduates at commencement in 1850. It represents the letter "T" in the alphabet: "Young Timothy / Learnt sin to fly," and shows a youth pursued by an upright wolf-like creature with forked tail. To the note is another attached by Mrs. Bianchi: "Sent over the morning after a revel—when my Grandfather with his lantern appeared suddenly to take Emily home the hour nearing indecent midnight."

The image for "H" that concludes "Deserted Shelf" was taken from the same *Primer*, printed by Edward Draper (Boston, 1777). The "Exit" sailboat image at the conclusion of "Sterling Park in the Dark" was taken from N. L. Stebbins's *The Yachtsman's Album* (Boston, 1896) and the high-resolution photo was obtained via the Library of Congress duplication services. "The Deserted Shelf" contains direct quotations from "Voyages" by Hart Crane (Anchor Books, 1996).

For word collages in "Sterling Park in the Dark," I used, among other sources, Goethe's *The Metamorphosis of Plants* (MIT Press, 2009), *The Variorum Edition of the Poetry of John Donne*, general editor Gary A. Stringer (Indiana University Press, 2005), *The Complete Letters of Henry James*, editors Michael Anesko and Greg W. Zacharias (University of Nebraska Press, 2014), *Druid Craft: The Writing of "The Shadowy Waters," Manuscripts of W. B. Yeats,* transcribed, edited, and with a commentary by Michael J. Sidnell, George P. Mayhew, David R. Clark (University of Massachusetts Press, 1971).

"Widows & Pariahs 2" appeared in the *Paris Review*. "Chipping Sparrow" appeared in *Poetry* magazine. Portions of "Sterling Park in the Dark" were previously published in *Bricks from the Kiln*, Volume 7, December (2024), edited by Helen Marten, Harriet Moore, and Matthew Stuart.

Thanks to Lacey Jones and Tessa Bolsover for editorial assistance with "Sterling Park in the Dark." And thanks to Catherine Brekus, Kenneth Minkema, Harry Stout for their shared essay "Agitations, Convulsions, Leaping, and Loud Talking: The 'Experiences' of Sarah Pierpoint Edwards" in the *William and Mary Quarterly,* 3d ser., 78, no. 3, July (2021).